BLOOD LINES & OTHER PLAYS

DRAMA

Kraftgriots

Also in the series (DRAMA)

BLOOD LINES & OTHER PLAYS
DRAMA

Chris Anyokwu

kraftgriots

Published by

Kraft Books Limited
6A Polytechnic Road, Sango, Ibadan
Box 22084, University of Ibadan Post Office
Ibadan, Oyo State, Nigeria
✆ +234803 348 2474, 805 129 1191
E-mail: kraftbooks@yahoo.com
www.kraftbookslimited.com

First published 2014

ISBN 978–978–918–188–9

= KRAFTGRIOTS =
(A literary imprint of Kraft Books Limited)

First printing, October 2014

Contents

By the same author

I. Drama

Stolen Future
A Parade of Madmen
Ufuoma
Homecoming
Termites
Beyond the Wall
Camp Hope
Night Rain

II. Fiction

Ol'Soja and Other Stories
Harvest At Sunset and Other Stories

BLOOD LINES

For Nigeria at 100.

Cast

CHIEF OGIE

ATUNNE ⎫

OGHOGHO ⎬ — HIS WIVES

OMOSEFE

EHIS — HIS DRIVER AND FRIEND

OSAS — OGIE'S SON

JUDE — SON

IYEKE — DAUGHTER

IST WOMAN ⎫

2ND WOMAN ⎬ — VILLAGERS

THE ENOGIE — KING OF UGHEGBE

1ST OLD WOMAN ⎫

2ND OLD WOMAN ⎬ — VILLAGERS

PALACE GUARDS

SERVANTS

OGIE'S UNCLE

BABA — A NATIVE DOCTOR

CULTISTS

LEADER — CULT KINGPIN

VILLAGERS, MEN, WOMEN, AND YOUTH

DANCERS, SINGERS, DRUMMERS, ETC

DISC JOCKEY

CITY FOLK, ETC

Part One

Scene One

A village market road. People amble their way to market, carrying an assortment of goods, foodstuffs, etc. It's morning. As lights come on, two women on their way to market are seen regaling themselves with stories of recent social events and happenings.

1ST WOMAN: Ah! *Osalobua!* Ughegbe will hear this! For so long Ughegbe has been sleeping, sleeping while the rest of the world forges ahead. The other day it was Uyi village. Before then, it was Akpo celebrating one of their illustrious sons. Or was it one of their daughters again? I have forgotten which one? In fact what I'm trying to tell you is that, it's high time. It's high time, my sister, ah-ah! *Wetin!* Even in your sleep you would hear the sound of celebration like rumour of fanfare from distant lands. But it's only next door. Poor common villagers next door who cannot boast half of what Ughegbe has. Is it the sheer size of our village? Our able-bodied men and women? Our youth? The greatness of our markets? How about our produce? Second to none.

2ND WOMAN: And yet nothing to show for it.

1ST WOMAN: Not anymore. Not anymore my dear sister.

2ND WOMAN: All thanks to Ogie. The Great Lion Himself. (*She raises a song and they both dance to it briefly.*)

1ST WOMAN: The third wife! Did you hear me? Third (*Counts.*) one, two and now three? Wife number three. Na *moinmoin?*

2ND WOMAN: Na money dey speak, my sister. It's a matter of cash. (*Laughter.*) Chief Ogie shall paint *this village and*

12

the outlying neighbouring villagers red. I know my man, *Ovwiyiemwen*. When he took his first wife, *chei!* It was great. People did not go to farm for a week. Market, *nko*? For where? Did you go?

1ST WOMAN: Go where? Uhn-uhn! I didn't o. Do you want me to miss out on the wedding of the decade, with all the food, drink and all? *Lai-lai*, thank you very much.

2ND WOMAN: Good a thing Atunne, his first wife, is from here. A girl of yesterday. Well-bred, beautiful angel, *ewo!* She shone like a million stars on her wedding day. She was the envy of all the girls. No, not all the girls. All the women in the village, including me, I must confess. You *nko*?

1ST WOMAN: What are you talking about, my sister? You're still asking me. I was green with envy.

2ND WOMAN: At your age?

1ST WOMAN: At my age, my sister? At my age? Who wouldn't be? With money like *san' san'* flowing like river *Ezenughegbe, Iyiemwen*, it's irresistible. Atunne was bedecked with the most expensive coral beads. Her traditional wedding attire was not borrowed like it's customary with poor folk. Chief Ogie had Atunne's and his own outfit specially sewn. He didn't stop there. All the officiating elders wore specially designed wrappers and shirts, complete with walking sticks, beads and all.

2ND WOMAN: How about the various dance troupes? Both those from our village and from elsewhere? Remember that specially composed song – (*They sing it and dance briefly.*) Ah, what a day, that was!

1ST WOMAN: My sister, I tell you it was wonderful. Each time I recall that event, my body still trembles as though I'm the one that got married that day. A few years down the road, it was round two.

2ND WOMAN: Wife number two. This time in far away Egbe village. Oghogho, his second wife, is something else. What a thing of beauty, *chei!* That woman, my sister, is fine, *uhm!* Sometimes, I ask myself: "Philo, do you call yourself a woman? Ehn, do you call this paltry figure of meager flesh, a woman?" *Hmm!* There are women and there are women! *We're women, old* women. And there are also *women.* Oghogho's one of the rarest breed. A woman formed with the richest clay by Osalobua in His happiest creative spell. Oghogho is a *beautiful* woman, *Ovwiyiemwen!* Even me as a woman, I just could not take my eyes off her well-formed full breasts.

1ST WOMAN: How about her *Ikebe?* Her buttocks, big and rippling like this – *[demonstrates]* Na *helele,* my sister. Everybody, I mean everybody was drooling with naked lust and animal desire. That girl is the most beautiful creature I have ever set my eyes upon. But Osalobua is partial, o.

2ND WOMAN: He is, my sister, or else, how can He create some people very fine and beautiful and complete. And others ugly, and... and bony and lacking like us?

1ST WOMAN: My sister, it's a strange world of inequality.

2ND WOMAN: It's more of injustice. It's unfair ah-ah. Just look at us: skeletons full of mouth. Is this life? Struggle, struggle, struggle everyday and nothing to show for it. While other people have everything. Just look at Chief Ogie and his family, ehn? See his two wives, Atunne and Oghogho. They are very easily two of the most beautiful women alive. They now live in the capital city. With money, cars, different kinds of food to eat, exotic drinks.

1ST WOMAN: What of jewelry? I hear Atunne and Oghogho have the largest caches of precious stones, gold and diamonds. Real *original* stuff, not *Ochaja* made. They are now chauffeur driven with maids and house servants waiting on them and anticipating their every need. What a life of luxury!

2ND WOMAN: And now, Chief Ogie is gearing up for wife number three. This time he is taking his wife from another village. The village of *Evwae.*

1ST WOMAN: I have my doubts about this one.

2ND WOMAN: Why?

1ST WOMAN: Evwae village! Hmm!

2ND WOMAN: What about *Evwae* village? Anything the matter? Aren't they human beings? Aren't they healthy? Do their women not have the normal appurtenances of reproduction? My sister, answer me.

1ST WOMAN: They do. They do. *Hmm!* My sister, do you mean to tell me you do not know our village and Evwae don't intermarry?

2ND WOMAN: Why?

1ST WOMAN: I don't know for sure. Or rather, I don't know the details. It's generally said that Evwae people are very diabolical and wicked. It is said that in ancient time, they had poisoned our river, leading to mass deaths. Ever since, our elders forbid our young people marrying their women and our women marrying their men. Water used in washing the feet cannot flow upwards to the head. It's forbidden.

2ND WOMAN: All these ancient tales. Good a thing Chief Ogie is changing all this rubbish. Ah-ah! What type of life is that? I won't give you my daughter. You, don't give me yours. Why? Because my great-grandfather told my grandfather and my grandfather told my father; and my father told me and I am supposed to tell my son... Osolobua! What type of life is that? Ancient feud whose origin is a matter of conjecture and hearsay and speculation. That was then, this is now. We are in a modern age. And change drives everything. So my sister, forget your misgivings. Embrace the new world that Chief Ogie is creating for us all. Aren't you proud and happy that Chief Ogie isn't from these neighbouring villages? That we own him? That he's one of us, bone of our bones, and flesh of our flesh? See how he, he alone has transformed our once dusty and poor village. Before, we didn't have electricity. Now we do have light. Before, we didn't have good roads. Now we have fine-fine roads smooth like a baby's buttocks. Many of our boys and girls are now gainfully employed. And many more are going to school. All of these, thanks to Chief Ogie. If now, he wishes to marry the woman that catches his fancy, should an ancient feud over nothing stop him? I am asking you, my sister.

1ST WOMAN: Hmm, my sister, you have a point there. Afterall, nobody knows whether or not this so-called feud is a fabrication.

2ND WOMAN: It's the handiwork of mischief-makers, I tell you.

1ST WOMAN: *Bo*, let Chief Ogie marry his woman. If anything, it will cement our relationship with Evwae. Come to think of it, Evwae is an emerging force in trade and commerce. The people are very industrious and open-minded. So rather than erecting walls, we should be building bridges.

2ND WOMAN: Like Chief Ogie is doing, *abi?*

1ST WOMAN: Yes, my sister. And as you know Chief Ogie is not only giving Evwae village a face-lift, he is also doing the same here in our village. Everyone is involved, young people and the old alike. Repair work going on everywhere. You can feel the buzz, the excitement of approaching festival. If only life in the village can always be like this... I feel like a young girl again, waiting for Sunday to come and ask my hand in marriage! If I, an old woman, feel this way, I just wonder how our youths are feeling right now.

2ND WOMAN: My sister, you read my mind. I can't describe to you how I am feeling right now. Nostalgia? Maybe. But something more special *[wipes her eyes]* I feel so... so sentimental.

1ST WOMAN: Indeed, my sister, indeed we must attend this wedding. I don't like to be told: "this took place, that took place". What are my eyes for? Decoration? For where? I must give my eyes food. Good food. This wedding is a scrumptious dish for the eyes, I dare say. And after that –

2ND WOMAN: The Big One!

1ST WOMAN: Absolutely! The installation of Chief Ogie as High Chief Ekpen of Eghegbe. (*They burst into song and dance ... slow fadeout.*)

Scene Two

Evwae Village. Late afternoon. The compound of PA OSULA, father to OMOSEFE, Chief Ogie's Bride. It's the wedding ceremony between Ogie and Omosefe, his third wife. Sitting prominently on throne-like chairs is the couple clad appropriately in traditional Bini regalia. They are flanked on either side by Chiefs, political dignitaries, and business associates. As lights come on, it is noticed we are witnessing the concluding parts of the ceremony as the master of ceremonies informs us.

MC: Thank you. Thank you ladies and gentlemen. Oh, what a wedding. This is the wedding of the century by all standards, I swear to God who made me. Ladies and gentlemen, once again I present to you Chief Ogie and Chief Mrs Omosefe Ogie, the newest, freshest and finest couple in town. Put your hands together. Put your hands together for this wonderfully favoured and blessed couple. The bride is in fact beautiful, isn't she? Who wants to contest that? Or who wants to throw her hat into the ring? Who wants to compete with her? Gentlemen, have you ever seen a more beautiful woman all your lives? Me, I haven't seen. Mrs Ogie, you are the finest. (*Addressing her Parents.*) Daddy and Mummy, you are the best. Ladies and Gentlemen, look at Mummy. Very charming, even in her advanced years. Like mother, like ... Everybody ...

ALL: Like daughter. (*General laughter.*)

MC: Now, now that the wedding ceremonies are over and done with, we shall invite the dance troupes that have come from all over the country to come and perform for the viewing pleasure of the newest couple in the whole wide world. Relax everybody. I say what? Relax. Yes, relax because "Rice and Stew Very Plentiful "*[Laugh]*. You shall eat and eat and eat; drink and drink and drink until you can eat and drink no more. But first thing first. DANCE, DANCE, DANCE!!! Now, the first group. You have the floor. Please let's keep to time. Thank you very much. (*A group of Bini dancers dances onto the stage and performs one or two numbers. Two or three more groups take the stage after the first troupe. A festive atmosphere marked by loud drumming and singing and dancing must be created on stage. Amidst all of this happy commotion, Chief Ogie and his new wife, Omosefe get up to dance and acknowledge the goodwill of guests. Chief Ogie is a huge, formidably-built six-foot-six handsome man, very affable and debonair. As the couple dances, people cheer wildly. (Fadeout.)*

Scene Three

A river path in the village. The two women of scene one are seen on their way to the river, chatting as they go.

1ST WOMAN: My sister, do you know it still beats my imagination that Chief Ogie is now the rave of the moment?

2ND WOMAN: How do you mean, my sister?

1ST WOMAN: Hmm, a boy of only yesterday... when was he born? I ask you, when? His mates are still lazing around smoking cigarettes and quaffing *palmy*. But he has got everything.

2ND WOMAN: I still don't know what you are griping about. You sound as though you are not happy with him. Or you are not delighted he is doing well. Is achievement now a crime?

1ST WOMAN: Hmm. My sister, you misunderstand me. You should know me better than that. Why should I be cross with him because of his success? His greatness is *our* greatness as well. My point is that, come to think of it, Ogie was once a little boy in our village, running about like every other little brat in dirty panties, his head covered with ringworms and rashes. Always with a running nose. I would chase him off our backyard at times when he came looking for toys and scrap to play with. Gradually he grew, going from primary school to secondary school. That year, the Common Entrance year to secondary school, how many of them passed? Six? Seven? Out of two hundred pupils from the local school. Those who failed disappeared, some into the forest, some into farms. Others simply disappeared even when they are looking at you, standing right before you, you wouldn't notice them, completely futureless. Anonymous. Lost. But not Ogie. Luckily for him, his father, a proud farmer that he was, supported him all the way. Not to talk of his mother's doting upon him. Their only son. Hmm, it's just like yesterday.

2ND WOMAN: Whenever he returned from college, everybody would go to their compound to catch a glimpse of him. Now, wearing clean clothes and sandals, Ogie would go about carrying his novels, reading aloud to his former schoolmates. He would perform poetry, jumping around, ducking like someone trying to avoid an arrow. Even then, as small as he was, girls, in fact, women were lusting after him. Remember that infamous incident?

1ST WOMAN: Who can forget it? Siweku was a shameless woman. What she did was indefensible. *Osalobuamwen!*

2ND WOMAN: People then said it was due to the age difference.

1ST WOMAN: Meaning what?

2ND WOMAN: Her husband, Erhan, was too old for her. A girl in the flower of her life, *hen?* A woman in her prime, full of fire and bursting with desire. Erhan could only stoke her fire but he could not feed the flames, Siweku needed a boy her age, someone strong like a well-whetted cutlass to meet her need.

1ST WOMAN: And she thought it was a school boy that could meet her need? A mere boy wet behind the ears. It's shameful.

2ND WOMAN: And she forgot that Erhan was a dreaded native doctor, famous for his medicine. For most people he held the power of life and death in his hands.

1ST WOMAN: Wasn't that why Siweku's parents gave her to him when Uyin, his first wife died? She was very beautiful but equally headstrong. She had made a scene when she was being led to his house. People thought Erhan would conquer her with his strong charms. Even after bearing him three children, Siweku still had other ideas.

2ND WOMAN: That woman had a taste for scandal. It's shameful. She lured the boy to bed and that was it. They both threw caution to the winds and just started carrying on like the Billy Goat and the Nanny Goat in the neighbourhood. It's shameful, my sister.

1ST WOMAN: Erhan was very upset. He could not be appeased. The boy's parents begged in vain. (*Shakes head at the memory.*) It's just like yesterday.

2ND WOMAN: Our people say tomorrow is pregnant.

1ST WOMAN: Indeed. But thank goodness, it's all in the past now. It's a good thing Ogie's parents were able to guide him aright thereafter. And he was able to finish secondary school and then went to university.

2ND WOMAN: Yes, o, my sister. They said he read *all* the books in the university here in our country. Such was his thirst and hunger for more books that he decided to travel overseas for more books. And when he got there, he read *all* their books and returned home with lots and lots of certificates and laurels. *Oyibo* people gave him many awards and prizes. Ah, that boy is intelligent, *bo*!

1ST WOMAN: I also heard that one university in our country gave him doctor!

2ND WOMAN: So he is now doctor? Hey… hey… hey!!!

1ST WOMAN: Not medical doctor. But Doctor of Books.

2ND WOMAN: (*Looking confused.*) Hmn, I don't understand that. But I like the sound of it.

1ST WOMAN: As you know, my sister, Chief Doctor Ogie is the *Oga kpatakpata* of the biggest bank in our country.

2ND WOMAN: That means he has a lot of money, *abi?*

1ST WOMAN: Lots of it, my sister. In fact, I heard his money is so much, it is more than the sand on a beach. Property, *nko? Hmm! Berekete!* Lagos, Abuja, Port Harcourt, Kano, even London and America. Chief Doctor Ogie has property everywhere. The Queen of England is his friend, *sef*. He and world leaders talk just the way you and me are talking like this.

2ND WOMAN: On phone, *sha.*

1ST WOMAN: Yes. But when he travels, he talks to them face to face.

2ND WOMAN: No wonder a lot of people attended his wedding. I am very pleased to know him. He is my brother, my brother, my brother (*They begin to sing and dance. Slow fadeout.*)

Scene Four

CHIEF OGIE's *house in the city. A palatial sitting-room furnished with the latest electronic gadgets, chandeliers, exotic sculpture, etc. Several doors lead to interior of house. It is late afternoon. Two or three boys, aged around seventeen and eighteen, are seen sitting operating laptops and Ipads; about five or six people are seen, some sitting, others standing. There is a preparatory atmosphere as though a festival is around the corner.*

OSAS: Mum, what again do you want ordered for you?

ATUNNE: Ehn... ehn, let me see... have you ordered the lace material?

OSAS: Yes, Mum.

ATUNNE: How about shoes? What type of shoes did you order?

OSAS: Leather. Pure Italian leather shoes.

ATUNNE: Hey! Leather *ke?* Do you think I'm a school girl?

OSAS: Mum, come over. Come see. I have pictures of the items here... clothing, shoes, jewelry, perfumes, name it. All here. (*Mother and son stare at screen of laptop.*)

OGHOGHO: Jude, you *nko*; hope you've ordered for us, I mean me and your younger ones?

JUDE: Yes Mum. I have ordered ten different dresses for five of us – you, me, Smart, Julie and Junior.

OGHOGHO: Good.

JUDE: I have also ordered ten different types of footwear – different materials, different textures, different designs.

OGHOGHO: *Shey* you know our sizes?

JUDE: Ah-ah, Mummy. What do you take me for? Dunce? We've been in this house together for years. Shouldn't I know the size of everybody's shoes? Mine is size nine; yours is seven, Smart's is seven...

OGHOGHO: Okay, okay. Check Dubai for me.

JUDE: Okay, Mum.

ATUNNE: Osas, please check Paris for me. I need some perfumes.

JUDE: Sure thing, Mum.

ATUNNE: I don't think I like this one... this material (*Pointing to screen.*) Change it.

JUDE: But I've already ordered it, Mum.

IYEKE: You guys should not forget me, o. Osas, let me tell you what I want. Are you listening?

OSAS : Go on, girl.

IYEKE: Now, listen –

ATUNNE: Iyeke, how can you talk to your elder brother like that. I've always told you: be polite. You children of nowadays; politeness is not in your dictionary.

IYEKE: Mummy, what have I said that's offensive?

ATUNNE: Impolite. Impolite.

IYEKE: I merely said "now listen". What's impolite about –

ATUNNE: Attitude, Iyeke. Attitude. Your attitude's not good.

OSAS: Okay. Okay. Guys, just chill out. Okay? Mum, I say drop it. Okay? You've made your point. Now Iyeke, order me. At your service, ha ha ha.

IYEKE: (*Sulking.*) Forget it. I'm no longer interested. Who even fucking care about your fucking chieftaincy bullshit?

(Leaving.)

ATUNNE: Iyeke. Iyeke come back here! I say come – this girl is growing wings. Not in this house. Not while I am here. Not to worry, I'll take care of that brat. Spoilt thing. It's her father's fault. Over-pampering.

OGHOGHO: Fathers and Daughters *(Laughing.)*

ATUNNE: You bet, Oghogho. Chief practically adores them, all his kids. As though his wives don't exist.

OGHOGHO: You know men, or rather fathers. They all are like that when they are seeking your hand in marriage, they literally worship the ground upon which you step. You're the cynosure. The whole world revolves round you. And that goes on until the first child arrives. And if it is a girl! Your own *don* finish. Your rival has come, the little, cuddly wife. He will stop buying you things. But woe betide him if he comes home one day without a present in hand for "my baby!"

ATUNNE: All hell would be let loose. No end to the bawling of the little brat.

OGHOGHO: *Na wa,* my sister. It's our lot. What can we do? (IYEKE *reappears, all dressed up.*) Hey, QUEEN IYEKE OF UGHEGBE!

ATUNNE: Now, where in the name of common sense are you going this hot afternoon? *Ehn, Ogbanje?*

IYEKE: See you guys later. *(Departs.)*

OGHOGHO: Atunne, it's okay. Don't take it to heart. It's part of growing up. They call it youthful exuberance.

ATUNNE: *(Raging.)* What type of youthful exuberance is that? I call it juvenile delinquency. Look at them. Digital children of the new age. Every time on the internet, surfing, browsing, Social media: Facebook, Youtube, Instagram, Twitters and all whatnot. That's where they pick all these horrible habits from. No respect for authority. Oghogho, was that how you and I were brought up?

OSAS: (*Interrupting*) Mum, sorry to interrupt. Come look at these. (*She goes.*) This one is two hundred pounds. This one is three hundred euros. These other ones are way too pricey.

ATUNNE: Have you ordered for all of us? You and me and your three siblings?

OSAS: Of course. But I'm thinking we should order more items. I like to be spoilt for choice, you know, Mum.

OGHOGHO: Like mother, like son. (*General laughter.*) Jude, don't be left out, o.

JUDE: But Mum, you trust me. Our credit cards are loaded. So, no cause for control. Everything's under alarm, ha ha ha.

OSAS: Jude, baba!!!

JUDE: My guy! If we can't go overseas right now, at least we can order *anything* we want, yes, o!

ATUNNE: Digital generation.

JUDE: That's us, mama. Tell you what, this chieftaincy thing in the village is going to be massive.

OSAS: Massive, man!

JUDE: Yeah!

ATUNNE: By the way, where's Omosefe?

OGHOGHO: She has gone out with *her* husband. (*They both laugh.*)

ATUNNE: Osas, please hurry up and place an order for all we need for this ceremony. And make sure all the items arrive on time. The chieftaincy ceremony is around the corner. I like being prepared way ahead of schedule. It helps me plan and organize things, my own way.

OGHOGHO: Not only you. Even me too. Jude, I hope our dresses, jewelry, perfumes, shoes, bags and other accessories will arrive before the weekend?

JUDE: Mummy, I don't know. I hope they do. They've all been paid for. So we're set for the Big Day in the villa!

(*Fadeout.*)

Scene Five

A guest house somewhere in the city. A well-appointed room, sitting at table eating small chops and drinking champagne, are Chief (Dr) OGIE *in casual wear and his long-time driver, EHIS. It is night time.*

OGIE: Jonah has got to be there, you know, Ehis. He just has to be in attendance at my coronation... well, installation as High Chief of Ughegbe. The first of its kind. And I am sparing no expense and leaving nothing to chance to see that the ceremony is a huge success. When I say a huge success, I mean the whole world must know about it.

EHIS: How can the whole world know about a common Chieftaincy title installation ceremony? You have started exaggerating again, Ogie.

OGIE: Why do you talk like an illiterate villager? This is the 21st century, man. Technology is the answer. Ever heard of television.

EHIS: Ah, who hasn't?

OGIE: Ehen! Cable and satellite television stations are expected to broadcast it *LIVE*! *LIVE* to the farthest reaches of the globe, Ehis.

EHIS: Hmm, that will be something.

OGIE: Yes. I've got everything worked out, to the tiniest details. But my greatest headache, as you well know is how to convince Jonah to attend. As part of the logistical arrangement, I have instructed some people in the village to see to it that the village is given a face-lift. I have given Enogie some money to enable him to pay the workers, the labourers, I mean all the hands to be hired to, for example, tidy up roads, bush-paths, river-roads, the markets, and the village square, near the palace. The venue of the occasion.

EHIS: Impressive, I must say. How about food?

OGIE: I've been waiting for that question, Ehis. (*Laughter.*) Food is not a problem.

EHIS: I know the village women would be falling over one another to get a look-in. You know they are all fantastic cooks?

OGIE: That's been taken care of.

EHIS: How? You mean you've hired all the women in our village? Eh... commotion! How could you - ?

OGIE: Nothing of the sort, Ehis. Have all the professional fast food sellers gone out of business? A number of them have been engaged to provide refreshment.

EHIS: Just refreshment? For a big ceremony? Haah!

OGIE: There you are. But you accused me of exaggerating. This time around, I caught you off-guard.

EHIS: So you mean to say proper food like pounded yam and *egusi* soup will be served?

OGIE: Yes and much more. Guests will be spoilt for choice. *Ogbono* soup, *Edikaikon*, *Oha* soup, *Ofe Nsala*, *Ewedu* and *Gbegiri*, *Tuwon shinkafa*, you name it. We are looking to titillate the taste buds and palates of everybody, serving you your favourite dish. So are you happy now?

EHIS: Happy? I can't wait. You know I love the good things of life. Good food, good music, fine wines, lovely environment. Lovely things generally.

OGIE: And beautiful women, ha ha ha.

EHIS: (*Stammers.*) I... I... I don't know what you are talking about, Ogie.

OGIE: Come off it. Quit fooling yourself, Ehis. You and I have been around for... for how many years.?

EHIS: About twenty years.

OGIE: No. More than that. I am talking about since our childhood.

EHIS: About fifty.

OGIE: I think so. Even in primary school you'd shown that part of your nature.

EHIS: Which part of my nature?

OGIE: Women.

EHIS: Ah, let's not go there, Ogie.

OGIE: *Oho!* See you now? You used to harass those tiny tots in our class. And I'm sure you still do.

EHIS: Harass little girls?

OGIE: No. Big ones.

EHIS: Have you seen me with women? Do I even have one in my house?

OGIE: Are you now saying you do not answer the call of nature in that regard? The truth! Nothing but the truth.

EHIS: (*Listlessly*.) Let's forget about that. It's not important to me. Women? *Hmm!* You have no idea, Ogie.

OGIE: Okay, o! Don't worry. One day I will catch you Saint Ehis.

EHIS: Nothing like that, saints are in heaven. We mortals can only sin and ask forgiveness of the wronged. For whom is it a well, my brother?

OGIE: *Hmm.* Eat. Eat. Or are you fed up? (*They eat.*)

EHIS: I am almost getting to my limit. How much food and

of different types you've almost killed me with! That's one thing I like about you. Maybe that's the reason why I've stuck with you all these years. Food. I love food and you make sure I eat my fill. *Oga*, thank you, o. This your Chieftaincy ceremony go serious. I swear.

OGIE: That's why I need Jonah there.

EHIS: You've told him, *abi*?

OGIE: What type of question is that? Of course, he's the first to be informed. Why is he the president of the country?

EHIS: Has he agree to attend?

OGIE: In principle, yes. But you know how it is. Unexpected state engagements and things like that.

EHIS: For you to get Mr President to attend any event, even church service, his security must be top priority, you know.

OGIE: Absolutely. That's been taken care of, Ehis. I'm in constant touch with our security people, particularly from the villa. Like I told you, I am sparing no expense for this event. It's one unique opportunity I must maximize.

EHIS: Ogie, don't be angry with me, o. But I have one question for you: why does this event mean so much to you? Afterall, you are already a Chief. Infact, you have many chieftaincy titles conferred on you by several kings in our country. Some for your philanthropy. Others for your business wizardry, your political connections and influence. I sometimes think if you enter politics nobody can defeat you.

OGIE: Ehis, Ehis! You've spoken well. And I thank you from the bottom of my heart. You see our people have proverb: you do not stand on one spot to view the world. Yes, I am a Chief. I am a holder of many titles from different tribes and ethnic groups. I try to help people and that in essence is my mission in life. Talking of politics, you know I am not too keen. I'm not a politician but a simple banker.

EHIS: A simple banker? The CEO of the biggest commercial bank in the country?

OGIE: Ehis, my brother, we must never be content with crumbs. You must always reach out for the stars if you must be one yourself. And that's why this ceremony is so important to me. I want to be the next Central Bank Governor. I know I am qualified for the job, experience-wise. But in our environment, as you know, it's never about qualification, or expertise. It's all about *connections*. Who you know. Or who knows you or both. Mr President and I go back, way back in time, to the early years. Even before we made our mark in our different lines of work. He's always been interested in politics. But me, it's always business.

Jonah owes me so much. I helped sponsor his election. Of course, this is for your ears alone. Okay?

EHIS: I understand.

OGIE: If I can get Jonah to attend my Chieftaincy ceremony, we – he and I – can then find some space to talk in private. I can then raise the matter of the Central Bank Job. We can seal the deal in Ughegbe in the presence of the Enogie, if possible.

EHIS: Maybe you should get the Enogie to confer a title on him for good measure.

OGIE: No. Jonah will turn it down. Our village is too small and insignificant to him. What's important is to get him to enter into a secret deal with me, to support my candidacy. You know, this chap from the other region is equally desperate to defeat me. I'm told he wants to destroy my credentials so as to have the job himself. That fox will stop at nothing to besmirch my good name and ruin everything I have ever laboured for.

EHIS: But it's a mere job. To serve the people. Why do people fight dirty and to the death like that, *ehn?*

OGIE: You do not know anything. Who is talking about service? It's all about power. Influence. Personal glory. And by the way, the Central Bank job is not a *mere* job. The Governor is as powerful as Mr President. You hold the economy in your hands. You see what I mean?

EHIS: I think I do now.

OGIE: So, because of the sensitive nature of the position, you need to lobby. Lobby Kings and Queens. Lobby Emirs, Obas, Obongs, Obis, and Lords, spiritual and temporal. You will travel through forests and deserts, consult with everybody who is somebody. Bribe this, tip that. Marry this, befriend that. And while you are busy marrying this and befriending that, bribing this and tipping that, you must never forget to clean up your act. No skeletons in your closet. Or else forget the job.

EHIS: How's that possible?

OGIE: What?

EHIS: To live without having skeletons in your cupboard? Is it possible?

OGIE: We try not to, my friend.

EHIS: That's my argument. It is impossible. Look at it this way. What if they decide to investigate your private life?

OGIE: Oh, more than your private life. Your entire life is brought under the microscope. Your childhood, your academic training, schools attended and certificates awarded. Were they earned or did you bribe your way through school?

EHIS: How about police clearance?

OGIE: That one as well. People want to be sure you do not have a criminal record. You did not rape a girl growing up. You did not break traffic rules and regulations. You did not appropriate public funds for private use.

EHIS: The family *nko?*

OGIE: The family is given the greatest attention. The belief is that a person who cannot take charge of his home should not be entrusted with such a responsibility.

EHIS: So one's wife or wives and children come under scrutiny as well.

OGIE: Absolutely. And you too. You're close to me. You'd better be careful. I fail, we all go under. I succeed, we all celebrate. That's it.

EHIS: *Na wa* o! (*Shuddering.*) This is more serious than I thought, Ogie. I hope you've drilled your wives and the children on how to conduct themselves in public? You can never tell who is watching you and for what purpose. People are bad, I tell you, particularly those who are close to you. That's why I'm always alone. Trust? It's not in my dictionary, *sam-sam, at all.*

OGIE: Life is a gamble. Like everything else. And you cannot completely do without trust. It's like walking the earth and fearing it will cave in under your feet any moment. You can as well stand still and rot away. Trust is a risk and it's worth taking because there's no other way, my brother.

EHIS: The party, sorry, the Chieftaincy ceremony is slated for Saturday next week, isn't it?

OGIE: Yes. And everything is set. I should get Jonah's word on his attendance latest tomorrow when we meet at the villa.

EHIS: I hope everything goes on according to plan.

OGIE: Thank you, Ehis. (*Slow fadeout.*)

End of Part One

Part Two

Scene Six

Months later, Ughegbe Village. As lights come on, the two OLD
WOMEN *are seen sitting under an almond tree in a wide
compound, breaking melon seeds and chatting. It is midday.*

1ST WOMAN: I still see that wonderful car that is as long as
a boa constrictor, slithering its way through Ughegbe. In
it were powerful people who run our lives far far away
in the city. The leader of our country, for one thing.

2ND WOMAN: The whole Chieftaincy affair has come and
gone and still you will not quit dreaming.

1ST WOMAN: Hmm, it's beautiful sights like that that make
an old woman want to stay on this side of the grave. No
one knows for sure what awaits one on the other side.

2ND WOMAN: You're right there.

1ST WOMAN: Each time I sleep I just can't help dreaming
of that day. The day the whole world came to our village.
It's several months ago but it's like yesterday to me. Ever
since, everyday I wake up, it's as though I am expecting
that long convoy of exotic cars and huge motorcycles
and horses. And that huge multitude of people from
goodness knows where. But it feels a little sad and
disappointing that it has come and gone. Years to come,
seen through memory, Chief Ogie's installation will feel
like legendary stuff.

2ND WOMAN: Like when an elephant gives birth.

1ST WOMAN: Even more spectacular than that, my sister.
Is it child's play to be able to bring the leader of a big
nation such as ours to a small back-water village like
Ughegbe?

2ND WOMAN: How about all those cars with lights, blinding lights making deafening noise *whao ... whao ... whao ...*

1ST WOMAN: And dogs. Big like bears and lions held on a leash by smartly-dressed policemen. So many security people carrying small-small radio which talked to them and to which they talked. I said to myself: "*Ehen!* Is there no end to oyibo witchcraft?" Here we are, killing one another's children and hindering the modernization of Ughegbe. But see what the white man is using his own witchcraft to achieve. Witchcraft pass witchcraft, *bo!*

2ND WOMAN: That's why our young ones desert the village immediately they leave school. They want to stay away from here as much as they can. Our people as you know hate progress.

1ST WOMAN: We hate progress indeed. Or maybe we define progress, differently, wouldn't you say?

2ND WOMAN: Honey is sweet and good, whichever way you look at it. Progress is like that. Whoever does not like a nice house, he or she should go and sleep in the bush. How did you feel seeing those dignitaries... ministers, government functionaries, big men and beautiful women? Wouldn't you love Ughegbe to always be festive and colourful like that?

1ST WOMAN: Of course, of course, my sister. I saw so many different styles of dressing. Headgear of varied forms and shapes. Eye-catching and breathtaking dresses. Chief Ogie's three wives were simply spectacular in their dresses. From their wonderfully-tied head-dresses, their blouses, wrapper, beads, handbags and precious stones. They were like banks walking, *Osalobua!*

2ND WOMAN: Their children, *nko*? They too were well-dressed. They sprayed money on their parents as they danced. It was wonderful.

1ST WOMAN: There was so much to eat and drink. *Ha!*

How could one person feed a whole village? Ehn! Well, I was able to help myself to several helpings of *foo-foo* and *egusi* soup... he... he... he... what a day!

2ND WOMAN: Me too. I really stuffed myself to bursting. I saw Mama Ikpomwosa and Iye Ivie carrying plates of fried rice and chicken to their houses. And that they did, several times.

1ST WOMAN: I won't tell you lies. I myself kept some chunks of fried beef away in my house. They lasted me days after the event.

2ND WOMAN: Frankly, I had wanted to join the other women to go and ask for more food and meat. But what I saw shocked me beyond belief. While the event was going on and everybody was having the time of their lives, with lots of dancing and singing. *Hmn*, a big fight was going on on one side of the compound. Chief Ogie's children were tearing one another to pieces...

(*Quick fadeout.*)

Scene Seven

Flashback: At the Chieftaincy ceremony. Drumming and dancing going on with the multitude in convivial mood. Gradually lights dim on this wassailing folk and pan slowly across the crowd to focus more assertively on OGIE's children on one side of the compound. As this happens, all music stops haltingly and the joyful noise is replaced by the angry voices of the children as they take on one another in a free-for-all. However, the fight is between ATUNNE's and OGHOGHO's children, and it is not immediately clear what the fuss is all about. Snatches of expressions such as: "Fuck you, Idiot!; "Your fucking mother's a dog!"; "You bastard, how dare you insult my mother?" "I will kill you and all your fucking folks, fool!", "Get your filthy hands off me; you thief" etc are overheard in the hubbub. As this goes on, stunned villagers are seen looking at the fighters and one or two men, apparently from the city are also seen filming the entire proceeding with Ipads or cell phones. Later, EHIS storms in, takes in the commotion briefly and disappears. He reappears soon after with CHIEF OGIE, dressed up in a new regalia as High Chief, in tow. Total confusion. Blackout.

Scene Eight

A few days later. In OGIE's *residence in the city. A room furnished like a boardroom. Night time.* CHIEF OGIE, ATUNNE *and* OGHOGHO *are seen quarrelling.*

OGIE: I have invited the two of you here this time of night when the children are all sleeping in their respective rooms. And everywhere is quiet and silent. I really want to talk sense into your heads, the both of you. I mean, it's a disgrace that two of you, my wives of several years, two of you who know me inside out, my strengths and my weaknesses... especially my vulnerabilities. Oh, *Osalobiamwen!* You women want to kill me. What haven't I done for you, *ehn?* What? Cars, gold, silver, diamonds, everything, I have given you. And where haven't both of you traveled to? Paris, London, the US, Dubai, South Africa, the Carribean, you name it. You've traveled the world with or without me. Money is not your problem. Each of you – and your children – are millionaires, not just in naira, but in pounds and dollars. I bought and built houses in your names. You have the documents. Or maybe you deposited them with your lawyers . Atunne.

ATUNNE: Sir.

OGIE: Oghogho

OGHOGHO: Yes, Chief.

OGIE: What sin have I committed against you? What's my offense? Tell me. I need to know right now. Because this nonsense has got to stop.

ATUNNE: Chief, it's Oghogho's fault –

OGHOGHO: (*Fires back instantly.*) It's all your fault, Atunne.

ATUNNE: It's your fault, you witch!

OGHOGHO: You are the cause of all the trouble in this house. *Azen dan!* Jealousy – Jealousy!

ATUNNE: Look who's talking. Kettle calling pot black. Chief, this witch you call wife... *hmm... hmm.* I don't want to say anything.

OGHOGHO: Say it! I say, say it, old mama *youngie.* You and your daughter, I don't even know who is more... more rotten, h*iya!*

ATUNNE: Look here, Oghogho or whatever your name is. Do not use your filthy tongue to talk about my precious daughter like that! No way! You leave my girl out of this. Leave Iyeke alone. Oh, you're envious of my daughter *abi?* She's beautiful and you're not –

OGHOGHO: Hey, stop there, Atunne! Who is beautiful?

ATUNNE: My girl, Iyeke. She is a beautiful girl (*Booing.*)

OGHOGHO: Is that... that slut beautiful? Can any man choose her over me?

ATUNNE: Who is a slut? Oghogho, I ask you again: who is a slut? (*Advancing menacingly towards* OGHOGHO. OGIE *interposes.*)

OGIE: Now ... now, women, control yourselves. I say control yourselves. You, go and sit there and you remain here. Here... not there. Here. Are you deaf?

ATUNNE: Chief, don't talk to me like that, especially in her presence, *ah-ah.* You are the one that does not make stupid people like this respect me.

OGHOGHO: Dem dey respect shit? You can as well go and buy respect in the market, foolish woman.

ATUNNE: You hear her? I'll teach this *thing* a lesson she will never forget.

OGIE: Now, stop this bickering, both of you. Stop, I say. I am the man here and you must realize that... ah-ah. *(Pause.)* I asked a simple question. This one said, "it is your fault" And that one shot back. "It's your fault!". Now I need to know why you two have decided to repay me evil for good. Why you two have decided to disgrace this family before the crème de la crème as well as riffraff in society. I need to know if you both planned to destroy me... me Chief ... no, High Chief Ogie of Ughegbe in the presence of the whole world. Begin to confess now. Starting with you, Atunne. Why this disgrace in Ugbegbe during my chieftaincy ceremony?

ATUNNE: Why always me? Let her confess first. She is the –

OGHOGHO: Hey stop it there!

OGIE: Atunne, you are wife number one. You start.

ATUNNE: Wife number one how? Is it because you married me before others arrived to ruin everything? Am I now your number one? Am I your favourite? By the way, where is Omosefe? The Apple of Your Eyes. Why is she not here? She should be here. *Shebi,* we are supposed to be confessing our crimes? Or did she tell you she's a saint? Oh, I see. We are sinners, she's a saint. So having children makes us sinners, and not having children makes one a saint? If that is the case, I love to be a sinner and be surrounded by *my* children.

OGIE: *(Nonplussed.)* What are you talking about Atunne?

ATUNNE: Go and bring Omosefe. She needs to know.

OGIE: I should go and bring Omosefe from her room. Wake her up from sleep and tell her: "Darling, Atunne sends me to you". What type of insult is this? Have I fallen so low in your estimation, Atunne? Am I no longer your husband, the head of this home?

ATUNNE: You tell me, Chief *(Hums a song.)*

(Pause.)

OGIE: And by the way, you also said "she needs to know". She needs to know what? Exactly what, Atunne?

ATUNNE: You tell me, Chief. Sorry, High Chief, ha ha ha…

OGHOGHO: You see, Chief. Are you still searching for the root of our trouble in the home?

OGIE: Atunne, why are you doing this? What's your grouse? How… exactly how have I let you down? You are my senior wife. The love of my life. We, you and I, started this family together when there was nothing. We suffered lack and poverty together. Until God changed our situation. You have access to my chambers more than anyone else in this house. Property-wise, you are head and shoulders about your co-wives. And the children. You *know* me, Atunne. No other person in this world *knows* me as much as you do. Is that why you want to hurt me? *Ehn?* Is that why you want to destroy me and ruin my career? Is marriage no longer for better, for worse"? *Ehn* Atunne?

ATUNNE: I don't know what you are talking about, Chief.

OGIE: Twenty years, for twenty years, Atunne, you and I have been living together as man and wife. It's true that Oghogho and Omosefe joined us later in this journey of life. it's our custom. That's family. The larger the better. And we have been happy. We are a blessed family. The envy of all. There is money. Lots of it. And children, too. This is a vast compound comprising several units of houses, sufficient for everybody. I could build a school and a clinic in our compound, if I so wish. We've got everything. So, Atunne, why do you want to destroy everything?

ATUNNE: Look, Chief. If you call my name again, I will walk out of this place. I'm even feeling sleepy. Look at the time. Nearly one o clock. You leave your favourite wife to be enjoying her sleep while you hold us hostage here. There is no form of indignity a woman will not suffer in this so-called man's world. No problem. God *de sha.* I think I will go on vacation abroad. Tomorrow, I am leaving this prison yard for you people. I need my peace of mind and freedom. Marriage is no bondage, *ah-ah.*

OGHOGHO: Atunne, so you don't even have one single bit of regard and respect for a man whose name you bear? It's a pity!

ATUNNE: Look at this one… (*Claps hands.*) *Hmn…* I don't have your time now. You know, you and me, we shall settle this. Woman to woman. I'm just going to tolerate all this foolishness until the right time. Water shall soon find its level.

OGHOGHO: (*Conciliatory.*) Atunne please…

ATUNNE: Hey, hey… hey… please yourself. Just let me be.

OGHOGHO: You know, you are my big sister in this house, ehn? Let's not fight now, Atunne. Sexy mama! (*Goes to her and sits on her lap like a baby.*) Please, big sister me! See your fine face. Your sexy eyes … your big hips …

ATUNNE: (*Thawing.*) Oooh - ! Please leave me alone, Oghogho. I'm tired. I'm tired of everything (*Sobs.*)

OGHOGHO: I am so so sorry, Atunne. Hmm, I'm sorry, now. Please, it's okay. Stop crying or else I will join you. I say stop crying.

ATUNNE: The pain, the pain. And the shame.

(*Silence punctuated by quiet sobbing by both women. CHIEF OGIE is at his tether's end. He paces up and down the room, fighting the tears. A Bini choral song from off stage floats in, rises to a crescendo. Fadeout.*)

Scene Nine

CHIEF OGIE's *special living room, tastefully furnished with various kinds of figurines and statuettes, showing his love for the arts. Adorning the wall are large-size art works and paintings. Dominating the wall facing the front door is a life-size sculpture of a Black Woman, nubile in its utter nudity. As lights come on,* CHIEF OGIE, EHIS *and* OMOSEFE *are seen chatting or discussing family matters among others.*

OGIE: You know Chief Oganga, don't you?

EHIS: Yes, Chief. I know him very well. Was he not the Minister of Oil and Gas who recently gave his daughter away in marriage? We were at the event, now. Have you forgotten?

OGIE: Good. Good, Ehis. I want you to carry those cartons in the store to his house. I have spoken with him. His security detail have also been briefed so you'll be allowed in.

On your way back, don't forget to pick up some soap and shaving cream for me at the Mall, okay?

EHIS: No wahala, Oga mi. Let me go now. See you madam. Okay Chief *(Departs.)*

OGIE: Yes. As you were saying ... you were asking me about ... what's it, again? My memory is failing me.

OMOSEFE: Chief, I have known this man for a long time now. But I can't claim to really know him as such. Who is he, really? He calls you by name, sometimes he calls you Chief, my Oga and ... it's like the two of you are playmates. It's unbelievable. Oga and his driver so intimate like that.

47

OGIE: Women! You people talk too much. Well, about him? Ehis is a wonderful character, for sure. You called him my playmate, you are right. In a sense, he is. Now, what don't you know already about him? Let's see... Ehis and I were formerly primary school colleagues in the village. He's the first son of Erhan, one of the herbalists then in Ughegbe. He's late now. I'm talking about his father, the native doctor. Way back then, Erhan was god among men. People dreaded him because of his alleged mystical powers. You know how bush people fear such things. Not that you'd blame them for their naivity, ignoramuses. They even fear night birds hooting on the Iroko. To them, these creatures are evil ... ha ha ... ha.

OMOSEFE: You were talking about Ehis, Chief.

OGIE: Ehis? Yes, yes. Where was I? Yes, I think ... yes ... yes ... Ehis and I in school way back. He couldn't go beyond primary school. Very brilliant, though and sharp-minded. But his father could not afford to send him to secondary school. Initially, he'd joined his father's line of work. Amateur *Dibie*, native doctor. But he couldn't stand the jeers and taunts of the girls in Ughegbe. "Baby wizard", they called him then. Suddenly, he'd disappeared from sight. Three years later, he'd resurfaced. A licensed driver. He went into commercial driving business. Shuttling between our village and Benin City. Whenever I came back from college then, Ehis and I would meet to share experiences. I would teach him what we boys called "vocabulary": you know, big-big words. Used to intimidate and impress girls. Our friendship has survived the passing years. When I needed a driver, he was the natural choice. That's it. It's been like that since.

OMOSEFE: And you also decided to build him a house in your home town. And harbour him here in one of our buildings.

OGIE: Yes. I need him around me. Close by. You talk, my

dear Omosefe as though you are not pleased he's living with the family.

OMOSEFE: Well, not that ... not that. But, Chief –

OGIE: Yes, my dear.

OMOSEFE: The man, I mean, Ehis is still single at his age. Is anything wrong with him?

OGIE: Why are you asking me that question? Am I his doctor? Look, I respect people's privacy.

OMOSEFE: As childhood friends and all, are you saying you've never bothered to enquire why your long-time driver is not married?

OGIE: A couple of times, yes. Like I said I hate to pry.

OMOSEFE: What did he say is the matter with him? Because, if you ask me, that man is every woman's fantasy. He is young or rather he looks quite youngish, fit, well-built like an athlete. Even his grey hair makes him more appealing. It's a wonder such a man is living all by himself. Alone in a BQ.

(Enter CHIEF OGIE's children.)

OSAS: Hi, Pops! Hello, Aunty Omo.

JUDE: What's up, Big Guy! Hi Sis Omo.

OTHERS: Good afternoon, Dad. Good afternoon, Sister Omo.

CHIEF OGIE: Hey, my troops! Where are you guys off to this afternoon?

ALL: The movies, Dad.

OSAS: Just stopped by to holler at you and Aunty.

OMOSEFE: Thank you, o. Wonderful boys and girls. Which film are you guys seeing today? I know you go there nearly everyday.

OSAS: You want to come with us? There's room in our cars,

you know.

OGIE: You guys go. Have fun. (*They hug him and* OMOSEFE *and depart.*)

OGIE: These children of mine never cease to amaze. Just the other day in the village, they caused such trouble. And now, look at them. They make you wonder whether what you saw was a figment of your own imagination. Wonderful children. I just love them.

OMOSEFE: *Hmn.* Talking about the show of shame in Ughegbe. How did you handle everything? Remember your friends were there. And your enemies too. By year's end, the nation hopes to get another Central Bank Governor appointed. And we are all hoping and praying, it should be you. At least, the President has assured you he's nominating you to the National Assembly. As a member of the ruling party, you shouldn't have any major problem getting the House to confirm your nomination.

OGIE: God willing. God willing, my dear. We can only try. And leave the rest to Him.

OMOSEFE: But I have been thinking. You may dismiss it as a woman's irrational whim. You know how you men reason.

OGIE: What's the problem, Omosefe? I do not joke with your opinion. You know that.

OMOSEFE: You said the driver ... your driver, Ehis, saw people filming the fight.

OGIE: I myself saw it with my naked eyes.

OMOSEFE: Hmm. So? Where does that leave us? Your rival for that post sent them. Pictures don't lie. Tomorrow you'll see them in the newspapers ... oh, my God ...

OGIE: *Oh* that? Relax, my girl. My boys have already taken care of those bastards. They and their goddamn videos, cameras and all are now history.

OMOSEFE: Meaning?

OGIE: Let's just say everything is back to normal. No cause for alarm.

OMOSEFE: Hmm. If you say so, Chief. You still have to caution your wives because I'm worried about their constant bickering.

OGIE: Caution them, how? Why?

OMOSEFE: Your wives ... (*Claps.*) *Hmm!* Those women you put in your home and call "wives". Well, I don't want to say anything. Sometimes I fear for you. I pity you.

OGIE: What is it again, this time?

OMOSEFE: Someone once famously declared that when a man marries once, his troubles begin. When he marries the second time, his troubles double. Like I said I pity you. And myself.

OGIE: Do I detect jealousy there?

OMOSEFE: No. I am not jealous. Jealousy is not one of my weak points. Chief, if you must be told. That fight among your children in Ughegbe was instigated by Atunne and Oghogho.

OGIE: Why would they do that?

OMOSEFE: How on earth am I supposed to know?

OGIE: So do not make silly and baseless insinuations, Omosefe. I love all of you equally. I cannot stand any of you sneaking up to me and talking rubbish. Do you hear me? And don't question my judgment and authority again! What ... what ... what nonsense!

OMOSEFE: (*Humiliated.*) Chief, is it me you are insulting like this? Am I now talking nonsense that I tell you to watch your back? You put enemies in your home and call them wives! You go out there daily and labour, morning to night. One meeting after another. Signing documents, formulating policy and all. But in your home, your so-called wives divert your money to their boyfriends and lovers! They are buying property all over the place for men who "service" them. You think your children were just fighting one another just like that? Atunne, the Chief architect of mischief and her partner-in-crime, Oghogho subtly encouraged them to make a scene there. They wanted to embarrass you. Take it or leave it.

OGIE: Now ... now, Omosefe. Now, let's lower our voices and take these issues one by one.

OMOSEFE: There's nothing to take one by one, Chief. I have suffered in silence in this... this circus for too long. I'm not going to take it lying down anymore.

OGIE: Look, Omosefe, I am your husband. Tradition stipulates that you as wife obey me in *all* things.

OMOSEFE: (*Curtseys sarcastically.*) Sorry o, my husband.

OGIE: Are you trying to insult me?

OMOSEFE: Insult you, *ke*? I dare not, Chief. All I am saying is: shine your eyes, Chief. SHINE YOUR EYES. What ruins the wall resides therein, my dear husband. I can't begin to tell you how many times I have caught your wives plotting against you. They even mock you behind your back. There is nothing they do not say about you. Decency will forbid me to utter such obscenities. You should have asked why your children misbehave the way they often do. Like mothers, like children, Chief.

OGIE: Don't worry. I shall put all these things right. Just let me finish with this Central Bank business. You know I have committed a lot of resources to this venture. It is costing me a lot of money, time and energy I cannot and will not allow anything ... *anything* or *anybody* for that matter to ruin my ambition. This job is very important to me, and it's my life.

OMOSEFE: *Ehen,* Chief. One more thing.

OGIE: Yes.

OMOSEFE: Are you not worried?

OGIE: Worried? What about?

OMOSEFE: How can you say: what about? Are you a child that I should use all my mouth to say it?

OGIE: Woman, relax. God's time is the best.

OMOSEFE: God's time is the best. God's time is the best. I am tired of being counseled like a baby. God's time is the best, time is going –

OGIE: What are you complaining about, ehn? Do you lack anything in this home? I mean *anything*? Look outside there. Many exotic cars for only you. Your wardrobes are full of expensive clothes and jewelry and shoes and bags. Everything. How many bank accounts do only you have? Ten? Twelve? You're richer than some local Government Areas. You alone, ah-ah.

OMOSEFE: Chief, to tell you the truth? All of these material things are useless to me. USELESS! (*Shouting.*) GIVE ME CHILDREN, CHIEF! GIVE ME CHILDREN!!! (*Begins to weep. Chief consoles her.*)

OGIE: Come on... come on, my dear. Please don't break my heart. Stop crying. Please. It's okay. It's alright. I'm also disturbed, *ehn... ehn,* my baby... God's time is –

OMOSEFE: Ehn-ehn! Don't go there. When you came for me, did you meet me defiled? I was a virgin when you married me. All my sisters, six of them have all given birth to many children. Only me. God, why me? Why me? Girls who married after me now have their own kids. Only me, God! Maybe, I should have ... oh ... God.

OGIE: You shall have your own children, I promise. Just give me time. You know I have a lot on my mind. I'm very busy –

OMOSEFE: Too busy to see the specialist? Ehn, too busy to go for check-up?

OGIE: I've told the doctor, I shall drop in one of these days, when I'm less busy.

OMOSEFE: He says I'm perfectly okay after they'd run all the tests. He insists you must come and do your own tests.

OGIE: Okay, okay. No problem. I shall do so, soon. Now stop crying.

OMOSEFE: I have a confession to make, Chief. Now, promise you'll not be cross with me.

(*Pause.*)

OMOSEFE: Promise?

OGIE: Promise.

OMOSEFE: Atunne and Oghogho, both of them have been bothering me. They urge me to get a boyfriend. They even pushed someone to me. And the guy is keen to sleep with me. Someone you know. Very well.

OGIE: (*Pretended anger.*) Who?

OMOSEFE: Uhm – uhm… uhm-uhm. I have promised not to tell.

(*Choral song offstage swells forth. Slow fadeout.*)

End of Part Two

Part Three

Scene Ten

Months later. The two WOMEN *of Scene One are seen by a streamside washing dirty clothes. It's late evening.*

1ST WOMAN: Have you heard?

2ND WOMAN: Heard what my sister?

1ST WOMAN: The city is boiling, o.

2ND WOMAN: How?

1ST WOMAN: Hmm! Who else is in trouble but our High Chief.

2ND WOMAN: What is it, this time?

1ST WOMAN: Wonders shall never cease, my sister. Some people said that armed robbers stormed his house and stole lots and lots of money. They said that the criminals brought trailers to cart away property worth millions of Oyibo money.

2ND WOMAN: *Heu! Osalobua!* Ehen! I thought they said it was hired killers who visited his home.

1ST WOMAN: No. it wasn't hired assassins at all. Because they did not kill anybody. Thank God.

2ND WOMAN: Hmm! We thank God for sparing their lives. The other day we were told his wives were fighting over property. Those women cannot wait for Chief to die before they start carrying charms and poison – for one another.

1ST WOMAN: We are here. Someone had better tell them. They can secure our services to help them settle accounts … ha … ha … ha.

2ND WOMAN: Who needs old women like us? Foreign

religions have made people cast aspersions on our kind. People do not believe in our mystical powers. The yearly bushfire ravages undergrowth but what can it do to the forest giants?

1ST WOMAN: We last like the earth itself. (*Pause.*)

2ND WOMAN: Is it true, my sister, that he wants to be the leader of our nation?

1ST WOMAN: Who?

2ND WOMAN: Who else?

1ST WOMAN: Chief Ogie?

2ND WOMAN: The same.

1ST WOMAN: I hear he is going for a big position in government. Which will be good for Ughegbe. But I also hear enemies are after him. See the robbery case, for instance. People say his enemies sent the thieves. If they had killed him. Imagine the way our people would have mourned him?

2ND WOMAN: The ancestors be praised for his deliverance. May our great departed not let us see misfortune. The world is deep ... Can I tell you another secret?

1ST WOMAN: What secret? That he entered into the village last night?

2ND WOMAN: Aaah! You've beaten me to it. But how did you know? I thought you were away to Agho village to visit Edede. Did you see him on your way back?

1ST WOMAN: Let's just say I'm aware he came. The walls have ears, remember?

2ND WOMAN: True. True. They said he came to see the Enogie about a very very sensitive matter.

1ST WOMAN: The top job?

2ND WOMAN: Maybe. Maybe not. But very serious and delicate ...

(*Slow fadeout. Flashback begins in the next scene.*)

Scene Eleven

ENOGIE's *palace. The* ENOGIE *is sitting on his throne, flanked on either side by a sword-bearing page and a scimitar-waving one.* CHIEF OGIE, *somewhat dishevelled is sitting on a chair facing the* ENOGIE. *It's night time and before the lights come on, we hear palace praise-singers intoning what strikes one as panegyric poetry telling of a proud past and, sadly, present chaos.*

OGIE: Your Highness. *Oba'atokpere.*

ALL: *Ise!*

OGIE: I'm in trouble, Your Highness. I am in deep trouble, Your Highness. My home cannot contain me any longer. Everywhere I turn, I see trouble. I see danger. And there's no one to trust anymore. Suddenly, I am like a beauty queen stripped of her dress in broad-day light in the marketplace. Naked, my Lord. I am now naked and I seek someone or somewhere to hide… to hide my shame, Your Highness.

ENOGIE: Now, my High Chief. What ails you? What's the matter that you fret like a chick bereft of its mother-hen?

OGIE: Your Highness. Thank you, your Highness for granting me audience. May you live long and may our village prosper under your able leadership. Enogie, you know my past. You know my history, Your Highness.

ENOGIE: What about your past? What about your history?

OGIE: Don't our elders say whatever is buried is buried? Do the dead bite from their graves?

ENOGIE: Who is after our High Chief? Speak plain.

OGIE: Your Highness, my enemies have discovered my greatest shame. The sole source of all my sorrows. And now, Your Highness, do you know the worst part? They are threatening to *expose* me to the world. Can you imagine that, Your Highness? Expose my shame. (*Quiet sobbing.*)

ENOGIE: How... how did they... your... those after you, how did they find out? This horrible past we've all put behind us? *Ehn?*

OGIE: I don't know, Your Highness. I don't know...

ENOGIE: And who are these evil-minded people intent upon wreaking havoc and spreading grief in the land? Who are they? Do you know them?

OGIE: I don't know their identity, Your Highness. Oh, I'm finished. Is this how my life's going to end? In shame and disaster? Your Highness, I am gone. I am finished.

ENOGIE: (*Chants briefly in Bini language.*) The world did not start today. There is always a solution to life's problems. Evil wears many faces. So does good. It's an eternal scuffle and our task is to seek balance and hope to achieve understanding. The world is deep. *Ehn...* who is there? Egiegie? (*From somewhere in the interiors of palace, a VOICE answers: "Your Highness"*)

ENOGIE: (*A young man appears and greets.*) Egiegie!

EGIEGIE: Your Highness.

ENOGIE: I want you to go and call Pa Ebeh, the native doctor. Tell him, the village is on fire –

EGIEGIE: Ah, the village? Our village?

ENOGIE: (*Ignoring him.*) Tell him he should be at the palace with the speed of a blink. Now go. (*Servant departs.*) Our High Chief, I feel your pain. We thought we'd buried the poison. How come we now taste it in our food? Pa Ebeh will be here soon. The oldest man in Ughegbe and the most reliable eye of the land. Whatever our children are doing out there in the roaring world, Pa Ebeh sees it all. And he tells us, if we need to know. Let me now confess this to you. Pa Ebeh actually hinted the other day that all was not well. That trouble was afoot. When I sought to find out exactly what he meant, you know how wily these old men are. He simply said: "Let's be watchful". He will soon be with us. And everything will be made plain as day. Now, what exactly do these bad people want?

OGIE: Only very recently, I started getting bad bad text messages on my phones. I have five lines, different networks, Your Highness. I think two or three of my lines are strictly for highly sensitive official and private matters. I don't give them out to people. Few people call me on those lines. But, Your Highness, these faceless foes have been sending me terrible SMS on all my lines!

ENOGIE: When you say terrible messages, what exactly are they saying in these text-messages? They want to kill you... they want to take your wives or kidnap your children... what are they saying, exactly? Tell us, we need to know.

OGIE: Your Highness, these people bombard me with countless SMS. Everyday. Morning, afternoon, night. Every time, my phones don't rest. They are urging me to give up my ambition to become Central Bank Governor. They say if I refuse to heed their warning, they will expose everything. Apparently, they were able to escape with some video of the fight among my children on my installation day. This is because, I was sent some pictures of that fight. And they claim they have more damning photos as well.

They also ask for money. Huge sums of money as "shut-up pay", as they call it. And most damning of them all, they know... they know of the arrangement. That people father my children for me ...

(Slow fadeout amid choral songs sung from offstage.)

Scene Twelve

Ughegbe *village. In* CHIEF OGIE's *ancestral home. Gathered together in discussion are* OGIE's *father, uncles, elderly men and young* OGIE *and a very young* ATUNNE. *One or two bushlamps are burning, placed on a stool. It's late at night.*

UNCLE: (*Clears his throat, total silence.*) My people, I'd like to greet you all for your patience and wise contributions to our deliberations. This is a delicate matter that has consumed our time for months and months. Ever since our son here informed us of his ... his em ... em ... let's say challenges, men in the family have not known a moment's sleep. Those who have shed quiet tears have cried, gnashed their teeth. We've all tried to keep it – I mean this rather delicate but by no means unheard-of issue. We have tried to keep it hush-hush. There are certain animals we do not share in public among old and young. This matter should never be shared with children or women. Not even Ogie's mother, if we can help it. As you all know, before we made the matter known to all of us, *men*, here gathered, we all swore an oath before Ogun, to keep it to ourselves and take it to our respective graves. My people, have I spoken well so far?

ALL: Yes. Yes. Our gods and ancestors are with you. Asien.

UNCLE: (*Continues.*) I thank you all, my people. (*Turning to* ATUNNE.) Emm ... my daughter. I want to salute you. I'd like to salute your courage. Not every girl these days is courageous like you, my daughter, Atunne. We've quietly gone about searching for a good and understanding girl like you. The gods themselves brought you to our attention. Not all missing objects are announced on radio or television. No. some missing objects, you look for them yourself, sometimes until your dying days. It is a foolish woman who washes her dirty linen in the village stream.

ALL: – Indeed
  – Indeed
  – Decency forbid!
  – That'll be shameful.

UNCLE: (*Pauses briefly.*) Our daughter. Whatever we do, shame keeps us on the path of decency. *Emm* ... Our son here, Ogie loves you. He says you are the girl of his dreams. And love overlooks all defects, my daughter. But before I continue, I would like to ask you one simple question. Atunne, do you love Ogie?

(*Pause.*)

ATUNNE: (*Voice hoarsened with emotion.*) I... do.

ALL: We didn't hear her. Speak clearly, daughter.

ATUNNE: (*Clears voice]* I said I do. (*General grunts of approval.*)

UNCLE: *Ehen!* Very good, our daughter. You see, life is full of ups and downs. And between husband and wife. What's important is natural love. And understanding. Since you and our son, Ogie love each other, we shall now proceed to the more sensitive aspects of our discussion. Emm ... our son has done well so far in life. He has acquired education, traveled overseas and amassed wealth. We can assure you, our daughter, we will take good care of you. Money is not a problem. Everything you want, we will provide, you will never suffer again in life. Bid poverty goodbye, forever. You shall never have cause to envy other women, either in this village or in the city. We do not boast in our family. Whatever we say we do. Now, do you have any questions for us, Atunne?

ATUNNE: I have one question, my elders. Since I've been

approached and told the nature of ... of the matter. Something has been disturbing me. (*Pause.*) Ehn ... I need to know: does it mean my husband ... I mean him and me will not *meet* like normal husband and wife? He will only eat my food and at night we will back each other in bed? Maybe someone else will do *it* with me?

(*Pause.*)

UNCLE: Emm ... I want to say thank you very much, my daughter, Atunne. You are a very wise girl, indeed. Your type is scarce. Emm ... to answer your question. Your husband shall not only eat your food, he shall also relate with you the way a man relates with his woman. Have no fear, then, he shall mount you and ride you to exhaustion. Emm ... the only little problem is that he might need additional help to make you a woman; to impregnate you. [*Pause*]. The problem's in the seed. The fact came to light when he went overseas. The white people tried their best. No hope. But let me quickly say this is not unusual as such. If I begin to mention the names of people who have had similar problems, day will break and we shall still be here. In our culture, we have ways of solving such problems. And this is one of them. So are you okay?

ATUNNE: I will like to ask one other question. Who will visit me?

UNCLE: Oh, that's straightforward enough. Very simple. We the elders have met and considered these matters. We've thought and deliberated long and hard about such issues. And all along, our son, Ogie has always made his own mind known to us. Regarding your query, our daughter, Atunne, our son would prefer you look for yourself a capable man. His job is to visit you, do the job and disappear. He's not to linger around you. You are a decent, self-respecting married woman. A wife. Our wife, not a harlot. And one more thing: our son prefers not to see or know the person. So extreme caution. Extreme caution and care must be taken at all times. My daughter, do you understand?

ATUNNE: Yes, Elderly One. *(Song offstage. Quick fadeout.)*

Scene Thirteen

In the city. CHIEF OGIE *in suit is seen in his plush office. He is extremely restless, pacing up and down as we listen in on his thoughts.*

OGIE: *(Soliloquising.)* So all these years, all these years, Atunne has been dating my enemies? Ehn, in spite of what my Elders said – what they told her. Explicitly. Go out there, far, far away from home and pick yourself a man. That's what they told her. That stupid woman, Atunne. They did not tell her to run about the whole place, sleeping around like a common prostitute with my enemies. Or, how else did my enemies find out ... ehn? Oh, my God! Women are devils! Particularly that witch called Atunne. Innocent-looking, all-smiling, harmless. And even stupid, I'd thought at the time. Atunne! Oh, my God! Is this how women are? Capricious? Callous? Traitors from their mothers' womb? Ehn? What didn't I give that woman? What? I gave her money. Lots of it. Houses, jewelry, connections, everything! She's traveled everywhere. Europe, America, Asia, Australia, the Carribean Islands, everywhere. With my money. She's even a Chief, like me. Everywhere they confer chieftaincy title upon me, she's always by my side. She too is made Chief. Just like that. How can I, a chief condescend so low ... so low like a pig to wallow in reckless sexual escapades like that? Is it not possible, she's the mole in the family? The informant. Hey, my God! This woman has killed me, o! Atunne is the devil in my home. She is the one behind all this *wahala*. All my plans, all my strategies, she will go and disclose them to my enemies. See now, Oghogho has joined her. Partners-in-crime.

God, how did I use my own hands to carry what will kill me, ehn? Women, women, you all are demons. Devils! Look at them, look at all the bastards they've gone to bring for me. Fathered by my enemies! See the way Osas behaves. Jude, Iyeke, all of them. I can't bear to look at them very closely. I just can't. What if I detect the physical as well as the behavioural traits of my enemies? These women will kill me. These women have killed me. Oh, my - ! I can't even challenge Atunne and Oghogho. My own wives! Ah! God, why is my life like this? What sin did I commit, that's unheard of? I have to do something urgently. I shall go down fighting to become Governor of the Central Bank. For me, now it's a matter of life and death, (*Enter* EHIS.)

OGIE: (*Addresses him.*) Oh, Ehis, how are you? You've arrived already?

EHIS: Yes, Ogie. What's cooking?

OGIE: Everything's fine, Ehis. So as we discussed, I have no desire whatsoever to go and consult a witch-doctor. Okay? I prefer a Pastor. A man of God, as they love to be called. So what's on your mind?

EHIS: Well, it's your funeral, Ogie. Not mine. I am just trying to help. After all, I'm just a driver, your driver. Not spiritual consultant. But if you ask me, my candid advice is that we go and see one baba that I know. He is very good. Even Pastors visit him for power. People looking for money, power, fame, children. They all troop to his house for solution, you talk about Pastors. You know how I feel about them. Most of them are fake. 419-ers. Haven't you been reading newspapers? All the bad-bad sins and horrible atrocities, it is Pastors that are committing them. Forget about miracles. It's film trick. These pastors are actors, I tell you.

OGIE: So what do we do? The President's already sent my nomination to the National Assembly for confirmation.

All things being equal, I should be the next Central Bank Governor.

EHIS: (*Hails him.*) CHIEF CHIEF! CHIEF CHIEF!! Please join me in welcoming the Governor of the Central Bank! (*Claps.*) Boy! Does that feel good!

OGIE: Absolutley, Ehis. Absolutely.

EHIS: Ogie, do you want your rival to beat you to it? Ehn? Look at what lengths he's already gone in trying to stop you. I know it's been very tough for you. Your success is my success, Ogie. And if you fail, we all suffer. That's it. As I was saying. This baba will give you protection charms. He will give you charms for favour. Which you need badly, if you ask me. Baba will cook you *sotay* nobody, I repeat, no one can eat you.

OGIE: Eat? Eat me?

EHIS: I mean, nobody can touch you. You become invincible. You know what the chameleon says?

OGIE: Forget about what the chameleon says. Or what the snake says. Just take me to this wizard.

EHIS: Baba is not a wizard. Baba is a native doctor. He is –

OGIE: Look, it's already 4pm. Let's go. (*Songs.*)

(*Fadeout.*)

End of Part Three

Part Four

Scene Fourteen

Deep in a village. Native Doctor's home. Night. As lights come on, CHIEF OGIE *and* EHIS *are seen sitting on the floor, actually on animal skin, yoga-style as* BABA, *looking weird and other-worldly, launches into a protracted song-story, searching, seeking ...*

BABA: My friend, what did you say was your name?

OGIE: Ogie, Baba, Ogie.

BABA: Ogie, hmm! The gods have spoken. They say you must befriend your enemies. The gods say you must embrace your declared foe.

OGIE: Me? Befriend that bastard who is vying for the position of Central Bank Governor with me? Baba, do the gods know to what criminal extent that beast has gone in his bid to discredit me? In his attempt to destroy all my achievements? Baba I can't. Tell me to undertake another task, even worse ordeals, I will. But to dip hands in the same plate with that ... that cobra, that rattlesnake, NEVER.

BABA: Why are you so upset by all that? That is to be expected, my friend. Life is war, so expect no favours from anyone.

OGIE: Baba, you don't understand. This guy from another region is the architect of my present troubles. Just go to social media and see all the rubbish he's been putting out against me? My family life is the worst targeted. If I have my way he will be dead. But if I kill him, it will be too obvious. People will easily jump to the conclusion that I did it. Because of the tussle over office. Just let me have the charms and the powerful amulets. Baba, I need, as I earlier told you, protective charms. Charms which guarantee favour. Serious *juju* that will make me formidable. Untouchable. And in charge, naturally.

BABA: My friend, you have no problem. I have already prepared all those charms. It's my job. And I'm going to give them to you. All that you seek, the gods shall give to you. And you will come back here to show gratitude. But first thing first: like I said, you must do as the gods command.

OGIE: Baba, I am ready and willing to do the gods' bidding.

BABA: I am delighted to hear that. On Saturday night, at about midnight, you will go to Eketeke Junction. There, a young man shall be waiting to take you to meet, finally, with your... shall we say enemy Number One or you may call him friend number One. It all depends on how you look at it. At that meeting, in the presence of the Great Souls of the land, you – I mean you and this person will embrace each other. You shall no longer be at loggerheads, but you shall reconcile your differences and become one. This is the message from the gods.

OGIE: (*Furious.*) The gods must be crazy. The gods must be mad. I'd rather die than–! Just what's the point? All of this, I can now clearly see, is going nowhere. And, Ehis, I hold you personally responsible for this foolery. (*Brings out wad of currency notes and drops it before the Native Doctor.*) Here. This is your money. I'm out of here. (*Storms out. EHIS and BABA share a knowing smile, fadeout.*)

Scene Fifteen

Days later. At the cultists' meeting, somewhere in the city. It is about midnight. In the half-light which lasts the entire scene, figures in red, presumably all male, are seen swaying to a special kind of music. The hall reverberates with different kinds of sound: some jabbering, and others, moaning as though in pleasurable pain, the whole place filled with "uhs" and "aahs", etc, etc. Lights-and-sound effects may be deployed to create an eerie and bone-chilling atmosphere. Later as the ritual builds up into a frenzy, the figures rearrange themselves into a semi-circle, facing the audience. Then, one of them gravitates towards their front, assuming leadership. If one looks closely one will realize this figure is clad in a more outlandish fashion than the rest. He is holding some rod-like projectile that looks like a mace. Earthenware pots of various types can also be seen placed at strategic locations. Bush lamps provide dubious illumination here …

LEADER: (*Speaking with authority.*) Great Souls of our land, I greet you once again.

ALL: All hail The Wise One. Respect.

LEADER: I say Great Souls of our land, I salute you!

ALL: All hail the Wise One. Respect.

LEADER: An important soul is joining us tonight *(They all grunt and growl in approval.)* A lost soul has come back home. This soul calls himself Ogie. Chief Ogie. We do not recognize any titles except the ones we bestow upon you. Other titles are useless. Meaningless. Now, Ogie, appear before the Great Souls (CHIEF OGIE *is led by another figure in red to the front. He is motioned to kneel. LEADER gives a sign and CHIEF OGIE is quickly robed like others by two members.*)

LEADER: (*Picks up pots.*) Here. Drink. (OGIE *hesitates.*) I say drink! (*He drinks.*) Take this. Drink. (*He drinks again.*) Now, take this. Eat. Yes, go on, eat, eat! (*He eats. Members rejoice.*) Now, you've drunk our blood and eaten our flesh. You are now one of us, Great Souls of our land. Let me repeat our Golden Rule to you again: ALL FOR ONE, ONE FOR ALL. That's our rule. Simple, isn't it? But it summarises everything. You rise in our group to become leader like me if you practise this rule diligently. But if you violate it, you die! A Great Soul cannot betray another Great Soul. It is forbidden. And, now to the business of the night. (*Hails.*) Great Souls of our Land!

ALL: All hail the Wise One. Respect.

LEADER: I say Great Souls of our Land!

ALL: All hail the Wise One. Respect.

LEADER: My second in command is here but is not here. The business of the night has necessitated his temporary absence. But he shall soon be with us. In due time. (*Calls.*) OGIE!

OGIE: Wise One, I hail you. Respect.

LEADER: Your initiation has just begun. You must also undergo a series of ordeals to truly belong with us. But you have started well. Your self-giving recommends you. Your future here is bright (*Members hail.*) But there is one obstacle. A major obstacle on your path to fulfillment. Hate. You must get rid of hate. Yes. You hate somebody. And that person is one of the Great Souls. My second in command. (OGIE *is nonplussed.*) Yes. I understand how you feel. Surprised? Shocked? I tell you, it's a small world. Yet, the man you hate; the man you consider an enemy is your friend. You indeed owe him a lot. Even your life. (EHIS, *clad similarly like others, appears.*)

OGIE: Ehis! What are you doing here? (EHIS *smiles.*)

LEADER: Yes. We are finally there. As they say, all that was hidden shall be made plain. And this is the hour. Ehis is my second in command. He is the so-called adversary you've been seeking to eliminate all these years. We know everything. But we shall not go into details. But let's just say, Ehis is the man doing your job for you at home. He is the father of *ALL* your children. And soon, your third wife shall give you a child. Thanks to this man. He is already hard at work on that score. (*Pause.*) But come to think of it. What does it matter who owns the child or who doesn't? Paternity is nothing. Parenthood is everything. Whatever we do in life we do it for the community. Community is supreme. The community owns the child. And who's the community but you and me? (*Pause.*) Now, Ogie, is Ehis your enemy? Or, do you regard him your friend? (CHIEF OGIE *rushes to* EHIS *and gives him a bear-hug.*) That is the spirit. Life is balance. All we seek is understanding.

OGIE: Thank you, wise one. Thank you so much.

LEADER: You are welcome. In the weeks and months ahead, you shall continue your initiation rites. We are happy the main obstacle is gone.

OGIE: Wise One, how about –

LEADER: The position you seek in our country. Yes, it's all yours. We decree it here. It is done out there.

OGIE: (*Falls on his knees.*) Oh, thank you. Thank you, wise one.

(*Slow fadeout.*)

Scene Sixteen

CHIEF OGIE's compound. It's evening. Crowd of people in convivial mood: A Disc Jockey is strutting his stuff on wheels of steel, regaling the dancers and merry-makers with the latest hit-tracks as CHIEF OGIE celebrates the senates confirmation of his nomination as Central Bank Governor. He can be seen towering above everybody, his wives, children, well-wishers, business associates, friends, relatives, etc. He is drinking champagne straight from the bottle as he moves around the crowd, acknowledging cheers and hugging and shaking hands. A loud banner hung over the dancing crowd proclaims the purpose of the occasion, i.e., HIGH CHIEF OGIE IS CENTRAL BANK GOVERNOR!!! HURRAY! HURRAY!! HURRAY!!!. NOTE: The Director to decide how long or short this celebratory scene should last before change of scene.

Scene Seventeen

Village. On the market road. The Two Old Women are returning from the village market, carrying baskets of food items, etc on their heads. Other people returning from market hurry past them, as they exchange brief pleasantries. It is nightfall.

1ST WOMAN: Today's market was wonderful. Fantastic bargain I had. Luck was footloose for me today. But guess who I saw at the meat seller's today.

2ND WOMAN: Mama Ikponmwosa? Iye Osamudiamwen?

(1ST WOMAN *shakes head "no".*)

Then who?

1ST WOMAN: Ehis, the son of Erhan. Chief Ogie's long-time driver from the city. They say he is visiting Ughegbe. He is here to see the Enogie. Looking young and fresh, that man never grows old.

2ND WOMAN: Grow old *ke?* How can he grow old when he is enjoying the good things of life in the city? If harmattan is ravaging the forest, do you expect the palm tree by the river to also wither?

1ST WOMAN: You have a point there, my sister. Hmm, but what I heard … or the message I heard he's brought to our Enogie is not good at all.

2ND WOMAN: My sister, tell it all. Tell it all. I'm dying to hear it. What are old women's ears good for these days but hearsay and gossip? Not that anything surprises me any longer. Not at my age.

1ST WOMAN: I thought you've heard it. The story was making the rounds in the market today. Hmm … wonders

78

shall never cease. Of course you know Chief Ogie was said to have landed his dream job in government at the highest level.

2ND WOMAN: Yes. Yes. We celebrated it in our village here, now, *abi?* We are all very proud and happy for him. At least, he is bringing and will continue to bring civilization to Ughegbe. So, what's it this time? What bad news has Ehis, son of Erhan, brought to our Enogie? That he is dead or what?

1ST WOMAN: They said he said that as people were eating, and drinking and making merry with him at his city home, all of a sudden, fire ... fire from nowhere started burning down his houses, cars, everything. People started running helter-skelter. Before fire-fighters could arrive, everything was gone. Only ashes was left. That's not all. Chief Ogie fainted ... or, I think they said he suffered stroke and has been flown abroad for treatment. As I speak with you, his wives and children have been put in police custody. My sister, the things that happen in this world, they are pregnant and are carrying a baby on the back.

2ND WOMAN: *Osalobuamwen? Iye! Iye!! Iyemwen!!!* My sister, I am short of words. Let's go home. See, darkness is falling around us ... (*They depart homewards. Choral song swells forth from offstage. Final blackout.*)

The End